The Serotonin Cradle

poems by

Morgan Boyer

Finishing Line Press
Georgetown, Kentucky

The Serotonin Cradle

Dedicated to Randall V. Boyer (1963-2012)

Copyright © 2018 by Morgan Boyer
ISBN 978-1-63534-599-5 First Edition
All rights reserved under International and Pan-American Copyright Conventions. No part of this book may be reproduced in any manner whatsoever without written permission from the publisher, except in the case of brief quotations embodied in critical articles and reviews.

ACKNOWLEDGMENTS

"Heroin" was published in *Rune*.
"I ate graham crackers, icing and M&M's" was published in the *Critical Point*. It was also the recipient of the Marilyn P Donnelly Award for poetry.
"My resume looks like a collage of random shit" was published in the *Pittsburgh City Paper's* online feature, "Chapter & Verse".

I'd like to thank my family, especially my mother Becky and older sister Alex. This would not be possible without them. I'd like to thank my professors Dr. Anne Rashid, Dr. Sigrid King, Dr. Louis Boyle and Jan Beatty. I'd also like to thank the Madwomen in the Attic, especially Daniela Buccilli for being such a great mentor. I also should thank Sandee Gertz Umbach, Andrew Mulvania, Dana LaSota, Pam Solmainy and Megan Wysocki. I'd like to thank Pressley Ridge and the Watson Institute. I'd like to thank Center Presbyterian Church, Church of the Covenant, First Presbyterian Church and Hot Metal Bridge Faith Community.

Publisher: Leah Maines
Editor: Christen Kincaid
Cover Art: Morgan Boyer
Author Photo: Morgan Boyer
Cover Design: Elizabeth Maines McCleavy

Printed in the USA on acid-free paper.
Order online: www.finishinglinepress.com
also available on amazon.com

Author inquiries and mail orders:
Finishing Line Press
P. O. Box 1626
Georgetown, Kentucky 40324
U. S. A.

Table of Contents

I. Prepare for the worst, and you'll never be disappointed.

I ate graham crackers, icing and M&M's for three straight days 1

Upon visiting my father's trailer park 2

My resume looks like a collage of random shit 3

Facebook Politics 4

Leg Cramps 6

A pile of black t-shirts 8

II. There's no such thing as a free lunch.

Southpoint 10

Sitting at the bar at my first anime convention 11

Heroin 12

Three Stages of Obsession 13

When I showed my father my childhood husband ... 15

Toy Truck 16

Confession 17

Souls of .jpeg files 19

The Serotonin Cradle 20

NOTES 21

I. Prepare for the worst, and you'll never be disappointed.

*"And they said I must be one of
the wonders, God's own creation,
And they smile as they can offer
no explanation."*
~Natalie Merchant, "Wonder"

I ate graham crackers, icing and M&M's for lunch for three straight days

in mid-December of 2007, Frau Gans' second period
German class of pimple-faced thirteen-year-olds
were hunched over Giant Eagle-bought boxes of Honey
Maid graham crackers on plastic desks in the room right

to the hallway between the cafeteria and the locker rooms
of boys who piled so much Axe body spray on their bodies
an innocent bystander could smell it two doors down.

Being the weirdo that I was, I brought in homemade icing in a Rubbermaid container with a red cap and a three bags of M&M's. If I remember correctly, the icing had six cups of sugar and about two cups of

2% milk from the Sunoco station across from the vet's office. Onto the graham crackers with a rubber spatula, like spackling mortar.

I sat in the left-most corner of the cafeteria at lunchtime with the leftover icing and M&M's. I dipped each one in like Intinction.

In my father's childhood trailer park
    "Nazareth! Can anything good come out of Nazareth?" ~John 1:46

a crumbling cardboard sign reads:

    "BEWARE OF dog BITCHES"

as if the man with his Sharpie
realized halfway through the various
ways it could be interpreted.

What a bastard of a poet. The barking
of his mutts, yaps of feral cats catch field mice

in their mouths walking
through the trailer park

like kings and queens
he leans over the interior

of a car's hood his unbuttoned
blazing red flannel riding up

his sweating spine as his
mutt trots to the wastewater

she just heard the cry
of her grandmother

who like her
was a barking 'bitch'

My resume looks like a collage of random shit

I stuck the first three letters of an author's last
name on the spine while stuffing a ham and cheese
sandwich in my mouth in a room
filled with Clinton-era *National Geographics*.

I spackled a Wilkinsburg woman's bathroom ceiling,
sorted piles of used bridesmaid's shoes in a non-profit
consignment store, yanked out forests of corn
stalk-tall weeds in beer-can-filled vacant lots.

I annoyed Westmoreland ski resorts by asking for their
addresses and phone numbers. Fighting the urge to
fall asleep to staticy, Nihilistic waiting music; Sharpies
that blacked out closed sub shops. Post-It notes with updated
websites of drive-in theatres in illegible indigo ink.

I spent my nights hunched over my computer in my dorm room
drooling like Pavlov's dog. While I masturbated to Dostoevsky,
my unpainted toes pushed up against my forgotten Biology textbook.

Facebook Politics
After Rankine

I've had a difficult time finding his work no matter which Carnegie library I check, but I have heard from his biographer that Atsushi Nakajima wasn't
anti or pro imperialist. He wanted to think about deeper questions than whether or not Hillary Clinton sent her emails to the right server, whatever sexist, racist garbage Trump said at a rally, or polls that have the lifespan of fruit-flies.

People acted like a stalker ex-boyfriend who sent me fifty Facebook messages and twenty texts every day.

A white woman in my art class screamed across the room: *If Bernie doesn't win the primary, I'm not voting!* and ranted on for forty minutes while all I wanted to do was finish the color theory assignment in peace. I wanted to get up and shout,

> *For Christ's sake, lady, it's ten twenty-two in the morning on a Wednesday, everyone's barely awake enough to be here! Sit the fuck down and shut up so the rest of us can work!*

I tried to say in the voice of a woman stuck working at the Wendy's Drive thru,
> *Ma'am, please be quiet, I'm trying to work.*

only to get a stern,
> *Don't talk back to me, young lady.*

Posts of memes and cartoons talking about transgender people assaulting little white girls' restrooms in South Carolina. Posts of videos about the stigma of tattoos and marijuana legalization. A friend's ex-boyfriend going on and on at lunch about how he's going to hide in a bunker if Hillary wins and calls her "female Hitler". An oil painting of Uncle Sam kneeling in prayer to the crucified Jesus.

I feel like a tiger, but not a free one like the one Nakajima writes about in *Moon Over the Mountain*. I'm one with a collar, watching as donkeys and elephants perform for the spectators tossing virtual peanuts at me.

His heart yearning for the mountains where he can be away from the chains of politics.

Leg Cramps

Paint palettes from
Rollier's Hardware Store
On the dining table near
the half-open box of saltwater

taffy as I fill out my
applications to work as a
cashier at Kuhn's. They're
one of the few grocery stores

that still have *homo-sapiens*
in every check-out line.
I go to sleep that night
on the Macy's outlet
couch downstairs at
two in the morning.

still livid from reading
the thirty-ninth chapter
of *Bungou Stray Dogs*,

it felt like I was on the
Kangaroo ride from Kenny-
wood but its JFK-era
controls never stopped.

I feel guilty about being born
in a time where that's my
biggest issue, not being

trapped in an iron lung in
a crowded hospital
dying in childbirth in my
mid-twenties, or living
below half-rotten
floorboards

of an unpainted stable
for months to hide from
the *Gestapo* in a Czecho-
slovakian village.

A quarter to noon, I
wake up with a cramp
in my calves. I feel like

everything I try flops over
dead like a plant that was
unwatered over a ten-day-
long vacation. I can't even
sleep on a couch correctly.

Piles of black t-shirts
    After Diane Seuss

Piles of black t-shirts with band logos;
    my trophy room carpet.

        Closet door seldom slid shut

Drawer-mouths hang open   sweatshirt-tongues

        Hamster muffles   carrots into her mouth-pouches

Mr. Boom-Boom   blasts music in his car outside
    he's the rave DJ   for fireflies and stinkbugs.

        pale blinds collects   spider webs

    Grinch decoration in my window
    when summer's nastiest mosquitoes bite

    Fruits Basket and *Dragon Ball Z* manga stolen
from Alex's bedside stand   atop a naked mattress.

        Jimi Hendrix   Alicia Keys CDs

stacked my dresser like   cheese   bacon
    onion rings   on a steak-burger.

    cassette tapes   disposable camera   a Serotonin
Brush   stray Legos   dully-sharpened pencils.

II. "There's no such thing as a free lunch." ~Randy Boyer

Southpoint

You'd always find the scariest looking person
in the room and try to make friends with them

at the tender age of 8   after ice-skating
            (or in my case, paying $20 to spend an hour
            of my life that I'll never get back continually falling
            on my ass   onto artificially-frozen water)

my mom took my sister and I to the pub upstairs
                nachos & cheese   chicken fingers
        fries   Cokes   as I munched on it   my attention
        turned to   four late   twenty-somethings
        surrounding   a pool table with cheap beers

        a skinny   A-cup woman   blond ponytail
        ripped   skinny jeans   black
        tank-top   multiple ear-piercings   eyeliner
        lower-stomach-area   Guns 'n Roses tattoo

As my mother   chatted with a coworker   I snuck over and
asked them   with my   "Boyer blue" eyes

        Can I join you guys?

My mother immediately   snapped out of the conversation
                and pulled me away
        Morgan, you don't know how   to play pool, come back here!
        Those are some serious players.   They don't want to teach
                some bratty kid how to play pool!

I sat with my head down in   our booth facing the window overlooking
            people who   paid $20 to fall   on their ass for an hour
My "Boyer blue" eyes glaring   processed cheese drizzled over the
        crunchy chips   ice cubes floating in my Coke-Cola.

Sitting the bar at my first anime convention

People in yellow   spandex suits
    sailor uniforms   a girl dressed
as Haruhi Suzumiya wearing a black bunny suit
carrying guitar   She reclined on a couch
    in the emergency exit hallway

an underpaid maid politely told her
    Ma'am, you're not supposed to have a real guitar inside.
Cracking a smile, the girl replied,
    I'm sorry, but are you trying to give orders to God?

I was taking bayou-swamp shallow breaths
    and cheap   rogue-colored cheeks

stuffing my face with meat   like a Uruk-Hai
sipping down Coke   as my mother was joking
    with a bartender and a Cloud cosplayer

Heroin
> *for Alex and the people of Washington County, PA*

Like spiders inside a shell of an abandoned babydoll
the baking-powder-looking substance sits by a needle

while policemen carry away a half-living woman
from the Walgreens employee bathroom floor.

a former mill worker sits with his grandkids, the flaking
white paint on his porch chips away with each passing day.

He and the other neighbors roll their eyes as they
continue to read the front page of the *Observer-Reporter*

another addict overdosed, stamp bags next to her, needle stuck in her arm.
Used syringes turning up name after name after name in the obituary

unfortunately for the former PTA board member on the uneven
tile floor, the angel of Narcan can't be in seventeen places at once

Three stages of obsession

I.   Nirvana

Your feet aren't walking on pillows
                                    they are pillows.

Your Global Gender Norms group   dumped
an entire Powerpoint presentation on your shoulders
                                      You don't care.

All you care about is the ticking clock to the next episode.

II.   Self-hatred

Your feet aren't walking cement
                                  they are cement.

You spent the night eating Cheetos and streaming Crunchyroll.

                Your friends invite you to lunch.
                                  You don't go.

You need to catch up on the Powerpoint your group
threw on you   at the last minute   You sit in the library
glaring at the dust on the monitor   wishing that you
were one of those tiny specs   that could be swept away.

All you know is that damn show's next episode is coming out today

                And you're going to end up watching it.

III.   Acceptance

It's been six months   beyond all odds and rationale
            you still like that damn show.
You added it to the ever-growing list of obsessions.

Like Romeo and Juliet   you're fickle and easily swept
off of your feet   Perhaps love at first sight
isn't dead   simply in a new form   You've found three
other shows that you've fell in equal love with and still stay
up until one to discuss   them with fellow fans.
God somehow decided   the world needed another
nerdy fangirl   who drinks Vanilla Coke
awaiting washing machine   to finish your darks.

Perhaps God decided   the world needed dogs
in the form of humans   we so often forget
the lessons   that animals teach us
                        only our toys are art.

When I showed my father my childhood husband

      a boy with periods
for pupils,   cocaine-colored
mohawk,   pointy,   pierced ears
and skin   the color
    of   lavender shampoo, he
was hesitant   at first
    in "considering"   him
      as a   "son-in-law"

I explained his allure: *Shin, the Supreme Kai of the East*

    Ten-year-old me thought
if I married him   I'd be the empress
     of the east corner   of the universe,
     an intergalactic Livia Augusta
     no longer the pale girl who ruins
her dad's   strategy games
     walking past with a blanket   destroying
      chips that symbolized   legions of
centurions trying   to conquer Britannia
     wiping out   the office light
that symbolized   Rome's sun
    in a   cardboard box.

I took my mothball-covered   blanket
     wrapped it   around like a cape,
     coronated   as empress,
despite tonsillitis
and a   102.3   Fahrenheit fever.

    No longer ill or confined
    to a plaid-skinned couch.

Five years after his death   we sold Rome's paper
      streets on Craigslist
    Who else can   understand intergalactic
    Roman politics   but a fucking genius?

Toy truck

> *In memory of Charles Kinsey, an African American caretaker who was shot while caring for an autistic man named Arnaldo Rios in Florida.*

the word *Autistic* comes onto the screen
in Elmer's glue white and discussions

about the toy truck "mistaken"
for a gun. In STAT camp, ACCLAIM,
and weekly social skills session,

in a sea of paste
Chantal was a young black
autistic woman with the voice

of a Met Opera soprano singer.
She wasn't a big talker during "socialization
time"; but when she did say something
aloud, it mattered and she meant it.

I think of her as I gaze at the TV;
the boy is sitting up, looking at the yellow
tape like he's inside a circus cage.

I can feel how the cameras must
pound him like a thousand
fast-pitched baseballs to the face.
How the sirens must be like

rusty screwdrivers jabbing
through his ear canal and how
much he wants to go
back to the world of his toy truck.

Confession

2007 was the year
Toaster, one of the tallest
boys (and the one
with the highest GPA) on the junior
lacrosse team tried to ask
me out when I was half-asleep
on my desk,
drooling over the
crossword puzzle
of our paperback
workbook. White board
of seven-syllable
words and vintage
posters of Rhine-side
castles and Berlin cafes.

I think the words
I told him was

What...wait...are you...talking about? Why are
you talking to me of all people? Let me sleep, please.

Perhaps Toaster practiced
in a toothpaste-splattered
mirror the night before, biting
his lip, tripping on his words
while his mom kept telling

him to come down to dinner,
his sister was yelling
at him to get out so she
could iron her bleached hair
and wash off her MAC mascara.

Whatever Toaster saw in
thirteen-year-old Morgan Boyer,
has been a mystery to
twenty-two-year-old Morgan Boyer.

Though maybe twenty-two-year-old
Toaster might think the same of his
thirteen-year-old self. Right now,
he's moving into his
apartment with his roommate
who he latched onto the weekend
of freshman orientation, going
through some seventh grade
photos as he unpacks bubble
wrap-filled boxes, coming across
his first confession.

Souls of .jpeg files

We purged   grandpa's
apartment   upon his
death   to meet Asbury's
deadline   to get everything
out of there   I was given

the task to scan all the photos
onto the desktop   I carefully
placed them out   of the creasy,
dusty Ziplock   bag   In the bottom

of the pack   was a photo
a pile of dead corpses, no
indication   of Axis or Allies
alignment   Just covered in burlap,
laid out like firewood
a barren   field behind them
marked   with tank tracks.

They were now simply a
          .jpeg file
          in a folder   of a computer
          belonging   to a girl that
          they've never   met, a girl
whose   grandfather
might've   been on the
          opposite side   of the battle

Perhaps even the one who killed them for all she knows. Seventy

Years   after the seaside
death   on an island
In   the Pacific,
they exist   as data

19

The Serotonin cradle

My eight-year-old-self,
stressed   from her
therapy session
       digged   skin into skin,
deep   like the blue
trenches with the neon-eyed fish
and   carnivorous algae.

I rocked myself in my Serotonin cradle.

My twenty-one-year-old self
huddles my dark   hairs prick
up when the art professor talks
about getting   *kids* involved
       in the cafeteria project.

Memories of being misled
by Carly Walsh to believe
       second-graders ate
kindergarteners   then left
me to pick at the track marks
       inside a plastic slide.

      My arms crossed as I
wait for my minimalist
       art piece to dry. My fingernails
dug into my   skin as I closed
my eyes.   My Serotonin cradle.

NOTES:

Page 1
Intinction is the Scottish Protestant version of Communion wherein a person goes to the pastor, takes a piece of bread and dips it in a cup served by an Elder, rather than the officers going around to each pew.

Pages 4
Nakajima Atsushi (1909-1942) was a Japanese author who wrote a short story called *Moon Over the Mountain*.

Page 6
Bungou Stray Dogs is a manga created by Asagiri Kafka that was adapted into an anime in Spring 2016 by Bones. It follows supernaturally-powered characters based on literary figures whose powers are named after their works.

Page 8
Fruits Basket is a manga created by Natsuki Takaya. It's one of the most popular **shojo** (girls') manga ever produced. It was adapted into an anime by Studio Deen in 2001.
Dragon Ball Z is a manga created by Akira Toriyama, who is currently working on its sequel series, *Dragon Ball Super* with his assistant Toyotaro. It was adapted into an anime by Toei Animation.

Page 11
Haruhi Suzumiya is the assertive, arrogant heroine of the 2006 Kyoto Animation series *The Melancholy of Haruhi Suzumiya*, based off of a popular light novel of the same name by Nagaru Tanigawa.
Uruk-Hai are monsters from the *Lord of the Rings* trilogy.
Cloud is the protagonist of *Final Fantasy VII*, one of the most popular installments of the series.

Morgan Boyer, 24, is an alumni of Carlow University. She received a Bachelor's of Arts degree in Creative Writing, with a concentration in poetry. She also holds a minor in communications. Boyer has been published in a multitude of journals; *Rune, The Critical Point, The Pittsburgh City Paper's "Chapter & Verse", Bridge: The Bluffton University Literary Journal, Linoleum,* and *Wilderness House Literary Review.* Boyer also received the Marilyn P Donnelly Award in 2017.

Boyer was diagnosed with high-functioning Autism when she was three years old. She also has dealt with grand-mal seizures since she was six. Despite these overwhelming odds, thanks to years of therapy she earned a Bachelor's degree with a 3.34 GPA. Boyer lost her father to kidney cancer, a survivor of the disease for eighteen years, when she was seventeen. Despite this, she carried forward to publish her first chapbook, *The Serotonin Cradle*, an exploration of a young girl's journey with Autism in the Rust Belt.

Boyer enjoys drawing, baking, playing with her dogs, listening to music, watching anime, and, of course, writing. Boyer is a member of the PC (USA). She is a passionate feminist who believes in intersectionality, especially when it comes to disabled and LGBT women. She also loves trees, chocolate, water and animals. Boyer currently lives with her supportive older sister and mother.

Boyer personally thanks you for checking out her first chapbook, and hopes that you enjoy it.

www.ingramcontent.com/pod-product-compliance
Lightning Source LLC
LaVergne TN
LVHW041522070426
835507LV00012B/1766